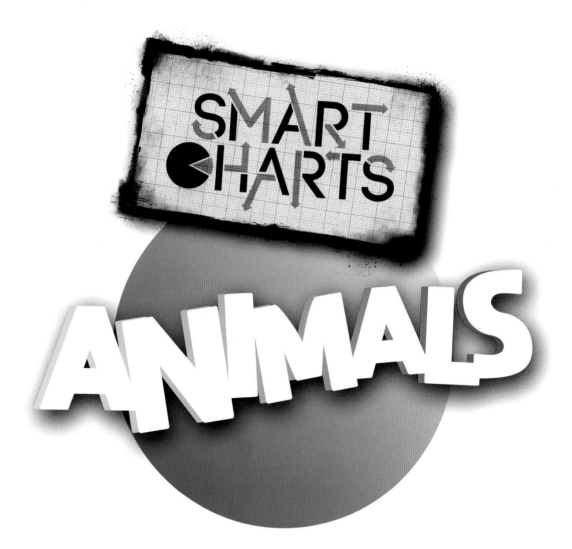

SMART CHARTS

ANIMALS

By Madeline Tyler

BookLife
PUBLISHING

©2019
BookLife Publishing
King's Lynn
Norfolk PE30 4LS

A catalogue record for this book is available from the British Library.

ISBN: 978-1-78637-450-9

Written by:
Madeline Tyler

Edited by:
Holly Duhig

Designed by:
Daniel Scase

All facts, statistics, web addresses and URLs in this book were verified as valid and accurate at time of writing. No responsibility for any changes to external websites or references can be accepted by either the author or publisher.

ANIMALS

SMART CHARTS

Words that look like **THIS** are explained in the glossary on page 31.

KNOW YOUR CHARTS!

WHAT IS DATA?

Data is another word for information. Data can be facts, numbers, words, measurements or descriptions. For example, someone might collect data about the different types of houses along a street. They might record how many houses there are, what colour they are, and when they were built. Data can be difficult to understand, or INTERPRET, if it's a long list of words and numbers, so people make it easier to read by showing it on a table, chart or graph. Different types of charts and graphs can be used to show different types of data.

TABLES AND TALLY MARKS

Tables are used to write down data about different things. They are usually quite simple and have a few rows and columns. Tally marks are used to count things up. The tally marks can be recorded in a frequency table. This shows how many of each thing there are. Tally marks are drawn in sets of five to make them easier to count. You draw four lines and then the fifth one strikes through the others.

HOUSE COLOUR	TALLY	TOTAL
RED	卌 |	6
BLUE	|||	3
GREEN	||	2
BROWN	卌 |||	8
YELLOW	|	1

PICTOGRAMS

You can use the data from a frequency table to make a pictogram. Pictograms show the same information but with pictures or symbols.

RED	⌂⌂⌂	6
BLUE	⌂⌐	3
GREEN	⌂	2
BROWN	⌂⌂⌂⌂	8
YELLOW	⌐	1

KEY: ⌂ =2

BAR CHARTS

Bar charts usually show data that can easily be split into different groups, such as colours or months. It is easy to compare the data in a bar chart to see which column is the highest.

y-axis
NUMBER OF HOUSES

x-axis – HOUSE COLOUR

Red   Blue   Green   Brown   Yellow

Graphs have two axes. The one that goes up and down is the y-axis and the one that goes left to right is the x-axis.

PIE CHARTS

10%
15%
40%
30%
5%

Pie charts are usually circular. They are split into different slices, just like a pie! Pie charts show data compared to the total number of something. For example, the total number of houses on the street is 20. Two of the houses are green – this is ten percent (10%) or one-tenth (1/10).

LINE GRAPHS

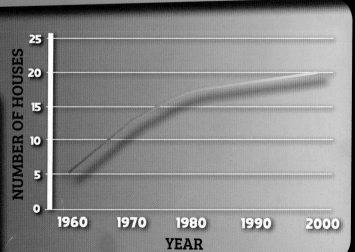

NUMBER OF HOUSES

YEAR

1960   1970   1980   1990   2000

Line graphs show if there is a correlation (a connection or trend) between two sets of data. This line graph shows that there is a **POSITIVE CORRELATION** between the number of houses and time – the number of houses has increased as time has passed.

ANIMALS

An animal is a living **ORGANISM** that belongs to the animal kingdom. There are billions and billions of animals on Earth, and they all come in different shapes and sizes. Some are tall, and some are small. Some are furry, and some are scaly. Some are fast, and some are slow. They all live in different parts of the world and eat different things.

Animals can be found on every **CONTINENT** on Earth, even the ice-covered continent of Antarctica. There are animals at the tops of the highest mountains, and at the bottom of the ocean. Different animals have different features and skills that can help them to survive in their **UNIQUE** surroundings. Animals can be sorted, or classified, into different groups based on where they live, how they look, or even what they eat.

Although they might all look very different to each other, ants, sharks, orangutans and peacocks are all animals. Even the spider under your bed is an animal!

Because there are so many different types of animal, it can sometimes be hard to make sense of them all and compare them with each other. Using graphs and charts can be a good way of comparing animals and seeing their differences more clearly. For example, you could use a pie chart to see where in the world the most animals live, or a bar chart to see which animal lives for the longest time.

WORLD TIGER POPULATION

POPULATION

120,000
100,000
80,000
60,000
40,000
20,000
0

1900 1910 1920 1930 1940 1950 1960 1970 1980 1990 2000

YEAR

Tigers are endangered, which means that they're in danger of becoming **EXTINCT**. The tiger population has fallen a lot in the last 100 years, but this line graph shows how it is slowly recovering and growing again.

CLASSIFYING ANIMALS

(KINGDOMS): Animals are just one group of living things that exist on Earth – there are also plants, fungi, protoctista and prokaryotes. These are kingdoms, and all living things belong to one of these five kingdoms. Sorting living things into kingdoms is an example of classification. Classification is when you group similar things together based on their features and characteristics.

(PHYLUM): If an animal has a backbone, like a parrot or a squirrel, it's a vertebrate. If the animal doesn't have a backbone, it's an invertebrate. Insects, octopuses and worms are all examples of invertebrates. Grouping animals into vertebrates and invertebrates is one way of sorting animals into their phylum.

Animal Kingdom

Does it have a backbone?

Yes .... No

Vertebrate   Invertebrate

MAMMAL   REPTILE   FISH
    BIRD   AMPHIBIAN

Vertebrate animals can be either mammals, birds, fish, amphibians or reptiles.

(CLASS): Although parrots and squirrels are both vertebrates, they're very different to each other. One has a beak and feathers and the other has a mouth and fur. The animals in a phylum can be grouped into different classes to show which animals are similar and which are different.

(GENUS AND SPECIES): Chimpanzees and bonobos both belong to the Pan genus. They may look very similar, but they don't belong to the same species, so they're not the same animal. Animals that share a certain set of characteristics and are able to **REPRODUCE** with each other are of the same species.

(DOMESTIC DOG):

Kingdom:	Animalia
Phylum:	Chordata (Vertebrate)
Class:	Mammalia
Order:	Carnivora
Family:	Canidae
Genus:	Canis
Species:	Canis familiaris

(FAMILY): Animals that look similar to each other, like mice and rats, usually belong to the same family. Rats and mice are very small **RODENTS** that have long tails, whiskers and pointed **SNOUTS**. They belong to the family known as Muridae.

(ORDER): Mammals can be classified into eight different orders. The order usually depends on what the animal looks like, what they eat, their size and their characteristics. Meat-eating mammals like lions and foxes belong to the Carnivora (carnivorous) order while small mammals with very large front teeth, like rabbits and hares, belong to the Lagomorpha order.

VERTEBRATE OR INVERTEBRATE?

There are around 60,000 different species of vertebrate on Earth. This might sound like a lot, but vertebrates only make up roughly 3% of all animals in the animal kingdom. This means that a massive 97% of animals are invertebrates! Most invertebrates, like insects, **ARACHNIDS**, worms and some **MOLLUSCS**, are very small. These invertebrates don't take up much space, so there's plenty of room on Earth to fit them all. You probably walk past hundreds of invertebrates every day without even realising.

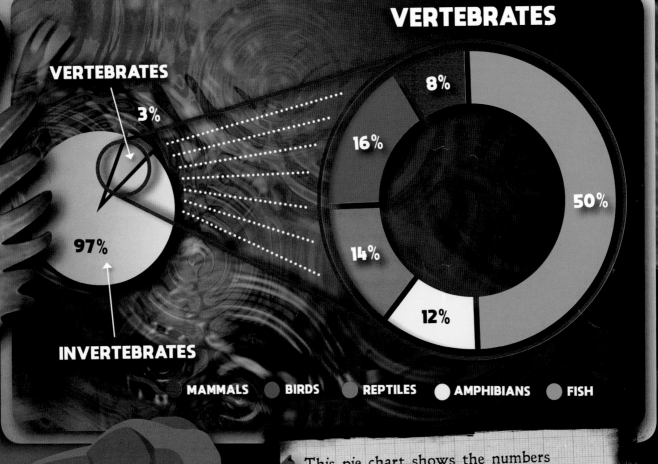

VERTEBRATES

VERTEBRATES

3%

97%

INVERTEBRATES

8%

16%

50%

14%

12%

MAMMALS   BIRDS   REPTILES   AMPHIBIANS   FISH

This pie chart shows the numbers of vertebrates and how some classes of vertebrates are more common than others. Half of all vertebrates are fish and only 8% are mammals.

NOCTURNAL OR DIURNAL?

Animals can also be grouped depending on how tall or small they are, whether they eat meat or plants (or both!), or whether they sleep during the day or during the night.

Humans are diurnal. This means that we are awake during the day and asleep at night. Unlike humans, most mammals are nocturnal. Nocturnal animals sleep in the daytime and wake up after the Sun has gone down. Most animals are either diurnal or nocturnal, but some are neither. These animals are cathemeral. Sometimes these animals sleep during the day, and other times they might sleep at night.

- ● CREPUSCULAR
- ● CATHEMERAL
- ● DIURNAL
- ● NOCTURAL

2.5%

8.5%

20%

69%

Some animals are crepuscular. This means that they come out at dawn, as the Sun is coming up, and dusk, as the Sun is setting.

WHEN DO ANIMALS SLEEP?

DAYTIME (NOCTURNAL)   BOTH (CATHEMERAL)   NIGHT-TIME (DIURNAL)

This is a Venn diagram. It can show if something, such as an animal, belongs to more than one group. This Venn diagram shows that lions and fossa can sleep both during the day and during the night because they are cathemeral.

FOOD CHAINS

Food chains tell us what different animals eat. They show us how all plants, animals and people are connected and how we all need each other to survive. Food chains start with plants. Plants are called producers because they use energy from the Sun to produce their own food. Animals are called consumers because they come next in the food chain and eat, or consume, plants and other animals. If something happens to one organism in the food chain, it will affect all the others in the chain.

GRASS → **RABBIT** → **FOX**

Although food chains are useful, they often don't show the whole **DIET** of an animal. Most animals eat, or are eaten by, more than one organism. Food webs show this by joining lots of food chains together.

ARROWS SHOW THE DIRECTION OF ENERGY.

FOX   **OWL**

STOAT

RAT   **RABBIT**

GRASS

Animals that hunt and catch other animals to eat are called predators. Foxes, owls, sharks and leopards are all examples of predators. Predators are usually very fast and have very good eyesight, sharp teeth or claws that help them to catch their prey. Predators are always either carnivores or OMNIVORES and are found at the top of the food chain.

Animals that are caught and eaten by predators are called prey. Prey are found closer to the beginning of the food chain and many of them are herbivores. This means that they only eat plants.

Some meat-eating, or carnivorous, animals don't hunt and kill their own food. Instead, they either steal a predator's catch or wait for a sick or injured animal to die before eating it. These animals are called scavengers.

CARNIVORES AND HERBIVORES

Animals eat all sorts of foods. Some animals eat meat, some eat plants, fruits and vegetables, and some eat a bit of both. Different animals need different types of teeth depending on what food they eat.

MOLARS

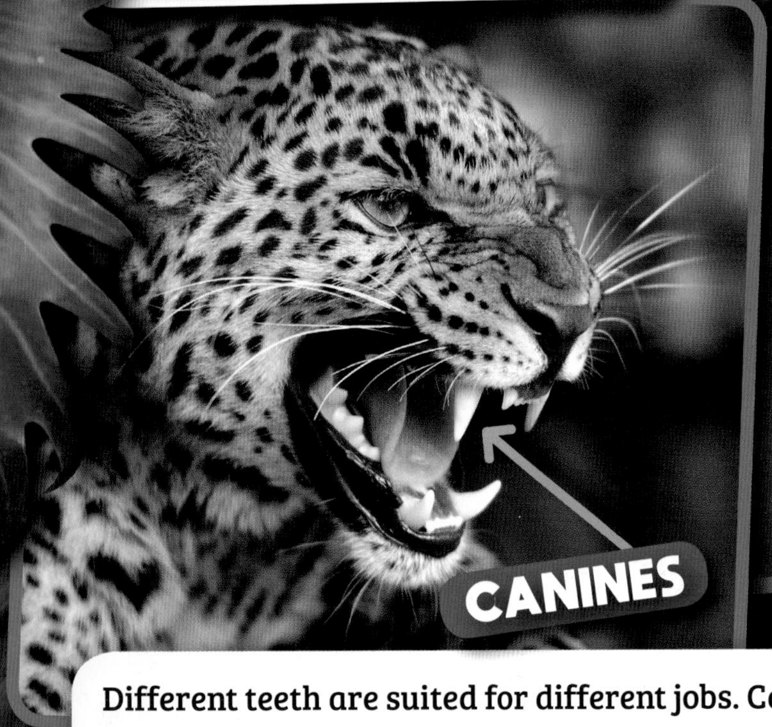

CANINES

INCISORS

Different teeth are suited for different jobs. Carnivores have sharp incisor and canine teeth that help them to tear and rip apart meat. Herbivores have wide, flat molars to chew, crush and grind the plants they eat. Carnivores have fewer teeth for crushing and grinding, and most herbivores don't have any canine teeth at all.

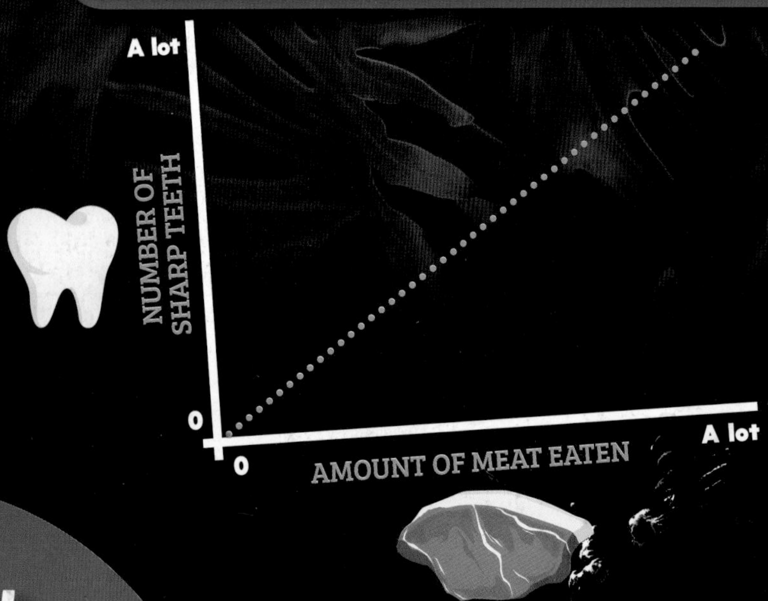

A lot

NUMBER OF SHARP TEETH

0

0

AMOUNT OF MEAT EATEN

A lot

The more meat an animal eats, the higher number of sharp teeth it needs to tear it apart. This line graph shows that there is a positive correlation between the amount of meat an animal eats and the number of sharp teeth it has.

Most animals eat the same thing every day, whether this is meat or plants. However, a few animals eat both meat and plants, feeding on anything that they can find. These animals are called omnivores. Omnivores aren't fussy, and most will try almost anything, as long as it's **EDIBLE**. They can move around and live in a range of different habitats or change their diet depending on what food is available.

The word omnivore comes from two Latin words: omnis (all) and vora (eat) – omnivores eat all the types of food on offer!

WHAT DO ANIMALS EAT?

MEAT (CARNIVORE)

BOTH (OMNIVORE)

PLANTS (HERBIVORE)

Hedgehogs, fennec foxes and pigs are all omnivores. They eat a mixed diet of meat and plants.

Not all omnivores have varied diets. Pandas live in the bamboo forests of China and, although they are omnivores, 99% of their diet is made up of bamboo. If something happened to the pandas' habitat, they would lose lots of their food and could starve.

WHAT DO PANDAS EAT?

1%

99%

- BAMBOO
- OTHER PLANTS AND MEAT

HABITATS

A habitat is the **ENVIRONMENT** that an animal or plant lives in. Habitats contain all the things that a living thing needs to survive, such as food, water or shelter. From deserts and rainforests to oceans and lakes, all habitats are different.

Different animals thrive in different habitats. For example, macaws live in the Amazon rainforest while reindeer prefer the frozen tundra of the Arctic and the taiga, or snow forests, of Greenland, Alaska and northern Europe. Animals are specially **ADAPTED** to survive in their habitats, so many species wouldn't do very well if they tried to live in a different one. Can you imagine a shark living in the desert? Or a lion living at the bottom of a lake?

Some habitats are a lot smaller than others. A microhabitat is a small part of a larger habitat. They have their own conditions which are different to the rest of the habitat. A fallen tree on the forest floor or a larger animal's fur are examples of microhabitats.

Water covers 70% of the Earth's surface and contains most of the world's habitats. Although only 30% of Earth is above water, this land can still be split and grouped into plenty of different biomes. A biome is a large area on Earth made up of lots of similar habitats. The CLIMATE in a biome is very similar and often the same species can be found throughout the biome.

EARTH

30%

70%

LAND WATER

LAND BIOMES

5%
2%
6%
17%
25%
20%
25%

GRASSLANDS   MOUNTAINS   DESERTS

TAIGA   RAINFOREST   DECIDUOUS FOREST

CHAPARRAL (SHRUBLAND)

There are seven main land biomes on Earth, and the largest of these are grasslands, mountains and deserts.

The largest biome in the world is the AQUATIC biome. The aquatic biome can be divided into two groups – marine habitats and freshwater habitats.

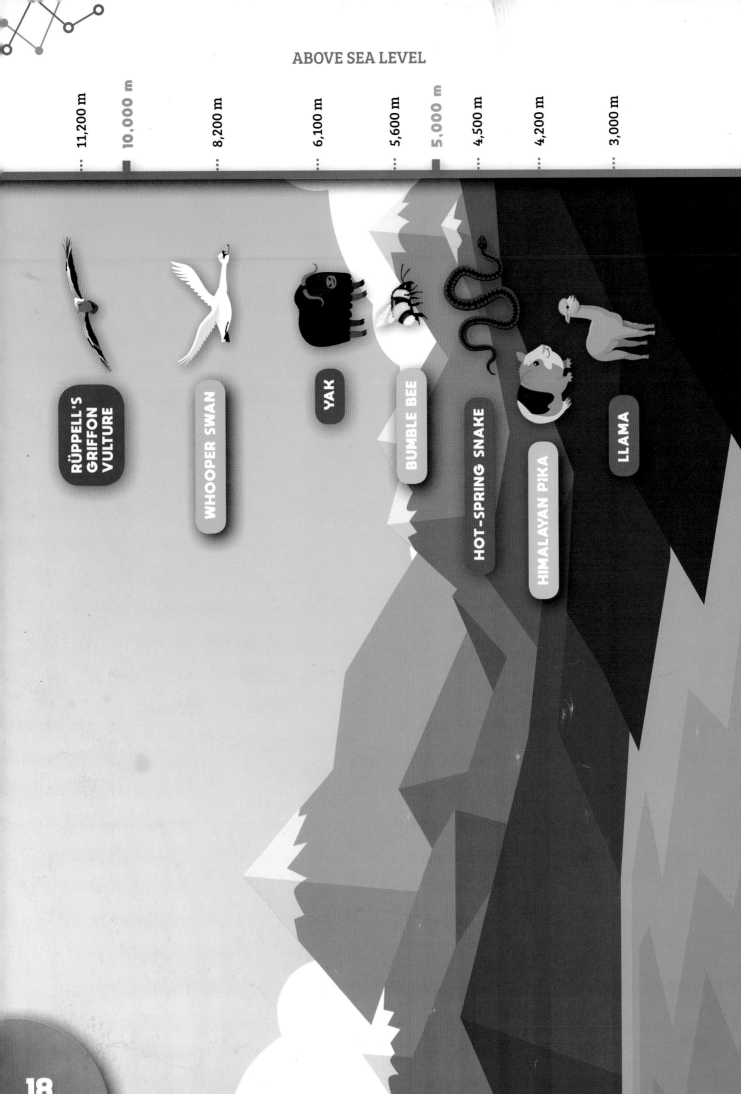

11,200 m

10,000 m

8,200 m

6,100 m

5,600 m

5,000 m

4,500 m

4,200 m

3,000 m

RÜPPELL'S GRIFFON VULTURE

WHOOPER SWAN

YAK

BUMBLE BEE

HOT-SPRING SNAKE

HIMALAYAN PIKA

LLAMA

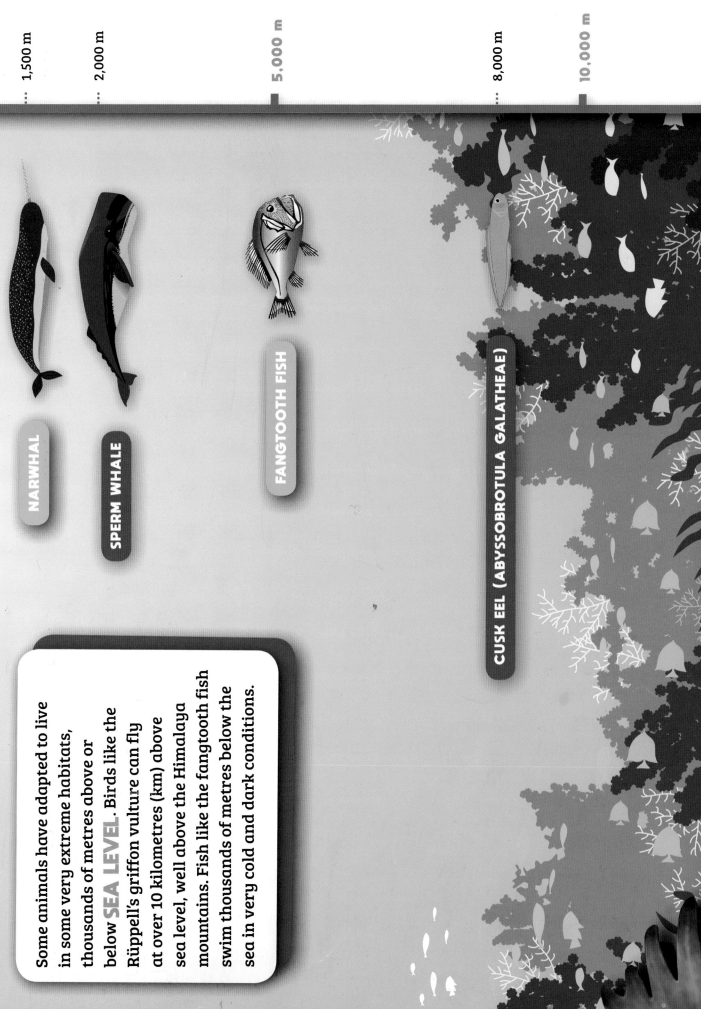

1,500 m

2,000 m

5,000 m

8,000 m

10,000 m

NARWHAL

SPERM WHALE

FANGTOOTH FISH

CUSK EEL (ABYSSOBROTULA GALATHEAE)

Some animals have adapted to live in some very extreme habitats, thousands of metres above or below **SEA LEVEL**. Birds like the Rüppell's griffon vulture can fly at over 10 kilometres (km) above sea level, well above the Himalaya mountains. Fish like the fangtooth fish swim thousands of metres below the sea in very cold and dark conditions.

19

ADAPTATION AND EVOLUTION

Animals have to adapt to survive in each habitat. A well-adapted animal will have special **FEATURES** that are suited to its environment. These features are sometimes called adaptations. These adaptations could be the way an animal looks (physical adaptation) or how it behaves (behavioural adaptation). Adaptations can help to keep an animal warm or cool, make it easier to run, swim or fly, or help them to hide from their predators or catch their prey.

The Arctic hare has lots of thick, white fur that keeps it warm. The fur also acts as a **CAMOUFLAGE** and protects it from predators.

Animals living in cold habitats have adapted to grow thick fur to keep them warm, while animals living in rivers, lakes and oceans, like fish, have adapted and grown gills that allow them to breathe underwater. Animals with the right adaptations are more likely to survive and pass these adaptations on to their offspring.

Although all members of a species are similar, there will always be some variations in their characteristics. For example, although all black-headed spider monkeys have a tail, some spider monkeys might have tails that are stronger or longer than others'. Spider monkeys' tails are very important because they use them to move around and swing between branches very high up in the trees. A spider monkey with a long, strong tail would find it easier to move between the treetops and, as a result, might be more likely to find food, escape from predators, find a MATE and reproduce than a spider monkey with a short, weak tail. Over time, more and more spider monkeys will be born with long, strong tails.

When a species changes slowly like this over a very long period of time, it's called evolution. Giraffes have evolved over millions of years to grow necks that can measure over 2.4 metres (m) long! These long necks allow the giraffes to eat from the tops of the acacia tree, where no other mammals can reach.

This line graph shows how giraffes' necks have slowly become longer over time.

THE SAHARA

A desert is a place in the world that only gets around 400 millimetres (mm) of rain every year. This could be somewhere very hot, like the Great Victoria Desert in Australia, or somewhere very cold, like the polar desert in the Arctic. Antarctica is the largest desert in the world, but the largest hot desert is the Sahara in northern Africa. The Sahara is home to lots of animals that have had to adapt and evolve to be able to survive in the **HARSH** conditions.

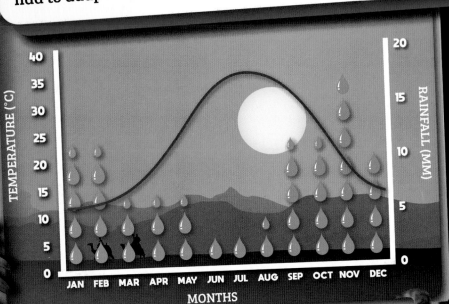

This climate graph of the Sahara is made up of a bar chart and a line graph. The bar chart shows how little rain falls every month, and the line graph shows the average temperature.

HORNED VIPER

Horned vipers are very well adapted to live in the Sahara. Their sandy colour helps to camouflage them in the desert. They use this camouflage to hide from predators and to sneak up on prey. Horned vipers are also nocturnal; they sleep during the day and come out at night when it's a bit cooler.

DORCAS GAZELLE

If it needed to, the Dorcas gazelle could go its whole life without drinking any water, which is very useful for an animal living in the Sahara. It gets all the water it needs from eating plants it finds around the desert.

EMERGENT
LAYER

CANOPY
SECTION

UNDERSTOREY

The Amazon rainforest is the largest rainforest in the world and is home to 10% of all known species on Earth. It's home to billions of plants, insects, fish, birds and mammals. The climate in the Amazon is very hot and **HUMID**: almost 20 centimetres (cm) of rain falls in the rainforest every month!

The Amazon is full of lots of dangerous predators that could eat the sloth if it's not careful. Luckily, because the sloth moves so slowly, green algae begins to grow on its fur. This acts as a camouflage and helps to hide the sloth amongst the trees.

Most lizards eat meat, but iguanas are herbivores. This is very useful in the rainforest. It means that green iguanas can climb high up into the trees, safe from predators, and feed on leaves, flowers and fruits.

Although yellow-banded dart frogs are small, they're very dangerous. Their skin is black and yellow which warns predators that they're **TOXIC**.

Zaparo's poison frog isn't actually poisonous at all! It's evolved to look just like the very toxic ruby poison frog to scare off any predators that may try to eat it.

MIGRATIONS

Not all animals live in the same habitat all year round. Some animals move from place to place to find food, water, or warmer weather. Other animals **MIGRATE** every year at the beginning of the **BREEDING SEASON**. This is called migration.

Salmon are born in freshwater but migrate to the sea soon after this. After a few years at sea, the salmon return to freshwater to lay their eggs. This is also called spawning. Some salmon swim up to 1,500 km **UPSTREAM** to spawn in the same place that they were born. Most species of salmon die soon after laying their eggs.

LIFE CYCLE OF A PINK SALMON

- EGG
- FRESHWATER
- SEA
- SPAWNING

LIFE CYCLE OF A SOCKEYE SALMON

- EGG
- FRESHWATER
- SEA
- SPAWNING

This is the life cycle of a pink salmon, or humpback salmon. They swim to the ocean almost as soon as they hatch from their eggs and spend most of their life here. Pink salmon only live for two years and die soon after spawning.

The life cycle of a sockeye, or red, salmon is very different to the life cycle of a pink salmon. They live for around three years longer than pink salmon and spend much more of their life in the river, lake or stream that they're born in.

Swimming 1,500 km may sound like a long way to migrate, but this is nothing compared to the distances some animals travel. The Arctic tern has the longest migration in the world at around 70,000 km! As soon as summer is over, the Arctic tern flies south from Greenland to Antarctica. After a few months when winter arrives, it's time for the Arctic tern to return north to Greenland. Migrating twice a year allows the Arctic tern to have a whole year of warm, summer weather.

Humpback whales have the longest migration of any mammal on Earth. During the summer, they can be found near the North and South Pole eating krill, but when **MATING SEASON** arrives, they swim towards the **EQUATOR**. The climate is much warmer there and is perfect for breeding.

ANIMAL MIGRATIONS

ANIMAL	
WILDEBEEST	
SALMON	
MONARCH BUTTERFLY	
LEATHERBACK TURTLE	
HUMPBACK WHALE	
GLOBE SKIMMER DRAGONFLY	
ARCTIC TERN	

0   10,000   20,000   30,000   40,000   50,000   60,000   70,000   80,000

MIGRATION DISTANCE (KM)

This bar chart shows some of the farthest migrations in the animal kingdom.

Although people aren't certain, many believe that the globe skimmer dragonfly has the longest migration of any insect on Earth. It's believed to travel almost 20,000 km every winter between India and Africa.

EXTREME ANIMALS

ANIMALS

1

2

3

4

5

6

0   0.5   1   1.5   2

SPEED (KPH

SLOWEST

If survival was one, long running race, then these animals wouldn't last much longer than a day. However, luckily for them, moving slowly can sometimes be just as useful as moving quickly. Moving slowly and steadily allows an animal to hide from predators and blend into its surroundings, just like the sloth does in the rainforest!

The slow loris moves so slowly through the trees that it's almost silent. If it senses a predator nearby, it can stay very, very still for a long time until it feels safe again.

Galápagos tortoises are some of the slowest moving reptiles in the world, only reaching maximum speeds of around one kph, which isn't very fast at all.

Starfish are a very slow-moving animal. They live in the sea and survive whilst barely moving at all. The fastest starfish can only manage around 0.03 kph – that's less than a kilometre a day!

What's the fastest animal in the world? You might be tempted to say the cheetah, but you'd be wrong. Cheetahs are the fastest land animal, meaning they can run faster than any animal on Earth, but there's at least one animal that can reach faster speeds. However, this animal doesn't run – it flies! The peregrine falcon can fly at speeds of up to 390 kilometres per hour (kph)! This makes the peregrine a very successful hunter and a deadly predator. When it's not hunting, the peregrine flies at around 65–90 kph. It only reaches its top speeds when it swoops down into a dive to catch its prey.

100 · 150 · 200 · 250 · 300 · 350

The peregrine falcon is not just the fastest bird on Earth – it's also the fastest animal!

Just like the peregrine falcon, the cheetah also only reaches its top speeds when it's hunting. Running at 120 kph uses up a lot of energy, so they can't keep it up for long. In fact, most chases are over in less than a minute.

At 110 kph, the sailfish is the fastest fish in the ocean.

HEAVIEST

Some animals are very heavy, and some are very light. The heaviest animal in the world is the blue whale. The blue whale isn't just the largest animal in the world, it's also bigger than any animal that has ever lived on Earth, including the dinosaurs! It can grow up to 30 metres long and weigh a massive 185,000 kilograms (kg)! Blue whales live in every ocean on Earth. Like humpback whales, blue whales migrate from Earth's two poles to water nearer to the Equator to breed.

816 KG **1,040 KG** **6,350 KG** **185,000 KG!**

WEIGHT (KG).

| 0 |
| 500 |
| 1,000 |
| 1,500 |
| 2000 |
| 2500 |
| 3,000 |
| 3,500 |
| 4,000 |
| 4,500 |
| 5,000 |
| 5,500 |
| 6,000 |

The African elephant is the heaviest land animal alive today and weighs around 6,350 kg. This might not sound like a lot compared with the blue whale, but it's still a lot heavier than anything else on Earth. They can grow to four metres high and eat over 130 kg of food every single day!

Kodiak bears live in Alaska and weigh up to 816 kg. That's around the same weight as 200 cats!

Crocodiles are the largest reptiles in the world. They can be anywhere between two and eight metres long and weigh up to 1,040 kg.

You might think that the heaviest animals also make the loudest noises. Although it does sometimes help to be bigger – for example, whales make some of the loudest noises on Earth! – it isn't always the case. Some of the loudest animals in the world are surprisingly small.

One of the loudest animals on Earth is the tiger pistol shrimp. The tiger pistol shrimp only grows to around five centimetres long and lives under the sea. The shrimp has small pincers on its legs which it uses as a weapon. It can close these very quickly to create an air bubble that heads towards the shrimp's prey at 100 kph. This creates a loud noise and a **SHOCK WAVE** that is powerful enough to kill the prey.

LOUDNESS IN DECIBELS (DB)

200	130	120	120	112	100
TIGER PISTOL SHRIMP	KAKAPO	HOWLER MONKEY	GREEN GROCER CICADA	HYENA	GREY WOLF

ANIMAL

Animals make noises for lots of different reasons. For example, hyenas 'laugh' when they have found food, while both grey wolves and howler monkeys howl to communicate with their packs and groups. Kakapo parrots 'boom' and green grocer cicadas 'sing' for the same reason: to find a mate.

ACTIVITY: GET SMART!

Go around your class at school and ask everyone what their favourite animal is. Make a frequency table of your results and use this to create a bar chart or pictogram. Is one animal more popular than the rest? How popular is your favourite animal?

ANIMAL	TALLY	TOTAL
TIGER	ⵏⵏⵏⵏ	5
HORSE	‖	2
RABBIT	‖	2
CAT	‖‖	4
PANDA	ⵏⵏⵏⵏ ‖	6
DOG	ⵏⵏⵏⵏ ‖‖	8
ELEPHANT	‖‖	3

Your frequency table might look a bit like this.

FAVOURITE ANIMALS

NUMBER OF PEOPLE

9 8 7 6 5 4 3 2 1 0

DOG   CAT   RABBIT   PANDA   TIGER   HORSE   ELEPHANT

ANIMAL

Which animal is the most popular in your class?

GLOSSARY

ADAPTED	changed over time to suit the environment
AQUATIC	to do with water
ARACHNIDS	a class of invertebrates that all have eight legs, such as spiders
BREEDING SEASON	a time of year when animals produce offspring
CAMOUFLAGE	traits that allow an animal to hide itself in a habitat
CLIMATE	the common weather in a certain place
CONTINENT	a very large area of land that is made up of many countries, like Africa and Europe
DIET	the kinds of food that a person or animal usually eats
EDIBLE	safe to be eaten
ENVIRONMENT	a person or animal's surroundings
EQUATOR	the imaginary horizontal line around the Earth that is an equal distance from the North and South Poles
EXTINCT	when a species of animal is no longer alive
FEATURES	parts of something
HARSH	severe and unpleasant
HUMID	to have a high amount of water
INTERPRET	to understand or work out
MATE	a partner (of the same species) who an animal chooses to produce young with
MATING SEASON	a time of the year when animals find a mate and reproduce
MIGRATE	move from one place to another based on seasonal changes
MOLLUSCS	creatures with soft bodies, no backbones and, usually, shells
OMNIVORES	animals that eat both plants and animals
ORGANISM	a living thing, like a plant or animal
POSITIVE CORRELATION	a relationship between two sets of data where they increase or decrease together
REPRODUCE	to produce young through the act of mating
RODENTS	small mammals with long front teeth, like rats and mice
SEA LEVEL	the level of the sea's surface
SHOCK WAVE	a wave of energy that travels through a material
SNOUTS	the front part of an animal that sticks out, including its nose and mouth
TOXIC	deadly or poisonous
UNIQUE	being the only one of its kind
UPSTREAM	against the flow of the current, towards the source of a river

INDEX